Our Wounded God

Beyond, Beside and Within Us

John Cullen

ISBN: 9781788126014

Designed by Messenger Publications Design Department
Cover design: Brendan McCarthy
Typeset in Adobe Garamond Pro and Goudy Old Style
Printed by Hussar Books

Messenger Publications,
37 Leeson Place, Dublin D02 E5V0, Ireland
www.messenger.ie

Dedicated to the Sisters of Nazareth

Introduction

Hands are a powerful visual for us in this book. When we look at the life of Jesus, we can see his hands raised in prayer: hands that heal, hands that bless, hands that restore sight to the blind, hands that feed the hungry, hands that shared meals with the least and the lost, with the Pharisees, with the disciples, with Martha, Mary and Lazarus; hands writing on the sand, hands open in welcome, hands that drive people out of the temple, hands washing the feet of the disciples, hands holding the lost sheep, hands commanding the sea and the winds, and hands that break the bread for a new and eternal covenant prayer of peace, presence and promise. We can name each one of the stations by the use of hands.

Contents

Opening Prayer

Faithful God, Jesus gave us his presence as food for our
pilgrim journey.
May our lives be taken, blessed, broken and given for one
another.
Jesus showed us a perfect love.
He gave us a new example to follow.
He calls us to serve to one another.
May our Way of the Cross
sustain, strengthen and send us out
to embrace you in the suffering ones.
We ask this, as a people,
redeemed and reconciled to God
through the blood of your Cross.
Amen.

But before his arms were outstretched between heaven and
earth,
to become the lasting sign of your covenant,
he desired to celebrate the Passover with his disciples.

(Eucharistic Prayer For Reconciliation – One)

The First Station:
Jesus Is Condemned to Death

We adore you O Christ, and we praise you,
because by your Holy Cross, you have redeemed the world.

Meditation: the hands of Jesus are tied

The Gospels remind us that Jesus said at the last Supper meal, 'One of you will hand me over'. This caused confusion among the disciples. This confusion is portrayed in Leonardo Da Vinci's Last Supper painting, where there is obvious uncertainty and puzzled faces among the disciples. In contrast, Jesus sits at the table with a calm serenity of waiting. Judas attempts to return thirty pieces of silver, saying, 'I have sinned in that I have handed over innocent blood.' None of the Gospels report that Pilate found Jesus guilty or condemned him to death or ordered him to be crucified. The Gospels report that Pilate 'handed him over to be crucified', or 'handed him over to them', or 'handed him over to their will'. The Gospels show us that Jesus was 'handed over' on three different occasions and by three different people: Judas in the Garden of Gethsemane, the leaders of the Pharisees, and Pilate at the end of a mock trial.

Reflection
... and, being rich in mercy,
you constantly offer pardon
and call on sinners
to trust in your forgiveness alone.
(Eucharistic Prayer For Reconciliation – One)

Scripture
Do not judge, and you will not be judged;
do not condemn, and you will not be condemned.
Forgive, and you will be forgiven
(Luke 6:37)

*Imagine if we dropped all grudges and
if the blood-stained tide of war in our world was stemmed.*

Prayer
Lamb of God, you take away the sins of the world, have mercy on us.

The Second Station:
Jesus Takes Up His Cross

*We adore you O Christ, and we praise you,
because by your Holy Cross, you have redeemed the world.*

Meditation: the hands of Jesus accept the cross

At the beginning of St Mark's Gospel, Jesus comes from Nazareth to be baptised in the River Jordan by John the Baptist. From this moment, events in Jesus' life seem to follow rapidly. The words 'immediately' or 'straightaway' are used eleven times! The pace of events is brisk as the story takes on a new direction of outreach. Jesus covers a lot of ground. He leaves behind him a trail of varied scenes: fishermen no longer at their nets, sick people restored to health, critics confounded, a storm stilled, hunger assuaged, a dead girl raised to life. Jesus' presence is active and transforming. Jesus saw people in need and he had compassion for them. He wondered at the unbelief of people in Nazareth. He knew that power had gone out from him when a woman touched the hem of his garment. Jesus is a person of initiative and decision.

Now, he takes the cross. He is no longer the subject of active deeds. Here, he is the recipient and the object of what is done: mocked, insulted, beaten, spat upon. Jesus is no longer the one who does – he becomes the one who is done to.

Reflection
'Never did you turn away from us
and you have bound the human family to yourself.'
(Eucharistic Prayer For Reconciliation – One)

Scripture
Then Jesus said to him,
'Put your sword back into its place,
for all who take the sword will die by the sword.
(Matthew 26:52)

*Today, our swords are long since beaten, not into ploughshares,
but into guns, weapons, tanks, bombs, bullets and missiles.*

Prayer
Lamb of God, you take away the sins of the world, have
mercy on us.

The Third Station:
Jesus Falls the First Time

We adore you O Christ, and we praise you,
because by your Holy Cross, you have redeemed the world.

Meditation: the hands of Jesus are weakened

When Jesus heals a blind man on the Sabbath, he says that the reason for the man's blindness is that 'God's works may be revealed to him' (John 9:3) and then he continues, 'We must do the works of him who sent me while it is day' (John 9:4). Jesus realises that his time for working is limited, 'night is coming, when no one can work' (John 9:4). At the Last Supper, Jesus says about the Father, 'I glorified you on earth by finishing the work that you gave me to do' (John 17:4).

The handing over of Jesus is associated with night. In John's Gospel, when Judas leaves the Last Supper to set in motion the betrayal of Jesus, he writes that 'night had fallen'. The phrase has a strong resonance: 'the hour' foreseen by Jesus had come, the time at which 'working' must give way to 'waiting'.

Now, Jesus is entrusted into several people's hands as his freedom is changed. He is pushed, whipped and jostled.

Reflection
Indeed, though we were once lost
and could not approach you,
you loved us with the greatest love.
(Eucharistic Prayer For Reconciliation – One)

Scripture
But many who are first will be last, and the last will be first.
(Matthew 19:30)

Disgrace is met with grace.
Blessings fall on those we curse.
We neatly place ourselves and others
on the ladder of promotion.
Service replaces status.

Prayer
Lamb of God, you take away the sins of the world, have mercy on us.

The Fourth Station:
Jesus Meets His Mother

*We adore you O Christ, and we praise you,
because by your Holy Cross, you have redeemed the world.*

Meditation: hands of comfort

The word 'suffer' has an immediate and inevitable connotation of pain, loss or distress, and it is where we derive the word 'passion'. To be faithful to the Gospel, we should reserve the expression 'the passion of Jesus' for that phase in his life when he was handed over to wait upon and receive the decisions and deeds of others, to become an object in their hands. What happens in the Gospels when Jesus is handed over is not that he passes from success to failure, from gain to loss or from helping to hurting. He passes from active doing to receiving what others do to him, from working to waiting, and, in the proper sense of the phrase 'handed over', from action to passion.

In this station, Mary sees what others have done to her Son, as they leave him diminished in stature, deprived of dignity and demeaned of respect.

Reflection
Help us to work together
for the coming of your Kingdom,
until the hour when we stand before you,
Saints among the Saints in the halls of heaven,
with the Blessed Virgin Mary, Mother of God.
(Eucharistic Prayer For Reconciliation – One)

Scripture
Blessed are you when people revile you and persecute you
and utter all kinds of evil against you falsely on my account.
(Matthew 5:11)

*God's presence is so humble, hidden and so invisible that it needs
an attentive, awake and welcoming heart to be recognised.*
(Pope Francis)

Prayer
Lamb of God, you take away the sins of the world, have
mercy on us.

The Fifth Station:
Simon of Cyrene Helps Jesus to
Carry His Cross

We adore you O Christ, and we praise you,
because by your Holy Cross, you have redeemed the world.

Meditation: hands of support

To people in their prime of life who are suddenly struck down by a serious illness or accident, there comes a particular moment when they recognise their need to help, and they are passed into the hands of others and become dependent on their decisions and actions. They now become a patient. A person who becomes a patient enters into passion. They become the focus of the decisions, care, treatment and therapy of others, who are often total strangers, like Simon of Cyrene, from a faraway country. They become aware of the dependence of their own destiny upon what is decided and done by others. This is the reason why some people become sensitive – to a degree that surprises and shocks them – to what the people who care for them do and say.

Simon the outsider quietly becomes part of the small inner circle of the followers of Jesus by carrying another's cross.

Reflection
Look kindly, most compassionate Father,
on those you unite to yourself
by the Sacrifice of your Son,
who heals every division.
(Eucharistic Prayer For Reconciliation – One)

Scripture
Give to the one who asks of you,
and do not refuse anyone who wants to borrow from you.
(Matthew 5:42)

The Giver of every good gift asks us to give.

Prayer
Lamb of God, you take away the sins of the world, have mercy on us.

The Sixth Station:
Veronica Wipes the Face of Jesus

We adore you O Christ, and we praise you,
because by your Holy Cross, you have redeemed the world.

Meditation: hands of compassion

A society in which homelessness exists will always be a 'two-tiered nation'. There is a distinction that will always remain between those who earn or achieve the wherewithal to live and those who receive it in the form of helping handouts. There are large numbers of people who share in the second category, living a life of economic dependence, which can tend also to generate psychological and social dependence. The elderly, the unemployed and the homeless are people who have become dependent on factors external to them. These factors are not controlled by their own efforts or initiative.

In our modern society, many people find themselves the receiver rather than the achiever of what is fulfilling. It has often been pointed out that advances in technology, with all its many positives, render people increasingly 'passive' rather than 'participatory'.

Veronica stretches her hands in a creative gesture, as she recognises the image of God in Jesus, though bruised and bloodied.

Reflection
Even more, by your Spirit you move human hearts
that enemies may speak to each other again,
adversaries join hands, and people seek to meet together.
(Eucharistic Prayer For Reconciliation – Two)

Scripture
You shall love the Lord you God … with all your heart
and your neighbour as yourself This is the reason why some
people become sensitive
(Luke 10:27)

William Butler Yeats called the heart 'a rag and bone shop'.
Who do we include and exclude from our hearts?

Prayer
Lamb of God, you take away the sins of the world, have
mercy on us.

The Seventh Station:
Jesus Falls the Second Time

We adore you O Christ, and we praise you,
because by your Holy Cross, you have redeemed the world.

Meditation: hands of courage

To 'work' for many people is to be 'a cog in the wheel'.
'A good day at work' is a day in which there are no major
problems, interruptions or failures. We all aspire to achieve
rather than receive, to be active rather than passive. In a way
this contradicts the modern cliché that our world has achieved
mastery of life beyond the wildest dreams of our ancestors.
Despite this mastery, our natural environment is under
perilous threat due to our mismanagement of it.

The complex environment of our modern society includes everything from underground fibre-optic cables to space satellites. All of our personal information is cloud-stored in computers. In today's world, we are not in charge. We receive rather than achieve.

Reflection
By the working of your power O Lord,
hatred is overcome by love,
revenge gives way to forgiveness,
and discord is changed to mutual respect.
(Eucharistic Prayer For Reconciliation –Two)

Scripture
… the measure you give will be the measure you get back.
(Luke 6:38)

'There is no one who cannot be helped by the prayer and the passion of Christ.'
(Pope St Leo the Great – Sermon 15 on the Passion, 3–4, Office of Readings)

Prayer
Lamb of God, you take away the sins of the world, have mercy on us.

The Eighth Station:
Jesus Consoles the Women of Jerusalem

We adore you O Christ, and we praise you,
because by your Holy Cross, you have redeemed the world.

Meditation: hands of solidarity

In the Gospels we see that Jesus was not a passive observer of people in the many different situations that he encountered. He initiated and transformed people's lives to give them a new horizon of hope. We read, not that Simon and Andrew were casting their nets but that Jesus saw 'Simon and his brother Andrew casting a net' (Mark 1:16). Also we read, not that the Spirit descended like a dove but that 'he saw God's Spirit descending'. Similarly we don't read that Matthew (Levi) was sitting at the Custom House, but that Jesus saw Levi sitting there. The Gospels see through the eyes of Jesus. The writers of the Gospels do not write that Peter, James and John went with Jesus up Mount Tabor, but that Jesus took them with him up the mountain. They do not write that the same three fell asleep in the Garden of Gethsemane, but that Jesus found them sleeping. The Gospels tell us that Jesus not only sees the women on the way to Calvary, but he responds to their presence and harvests their tears in his wounded heart, by speaking to them, 'do not weep for me, but weep for yourselves and for your children' (Luke 23:28).

Reflection
You brought us back to be reconciled,
so that converted at last to you,
we might love one another.
(Eucharistic Prayers For Reconciliation – Two)

Scripture
Jesus, looking at him, loved him and said,
'You lack one thing; go, sell what you own, and give the
money to the poor,
and you will have treasure in heaven; then come, follow me.'
(Mark 10:21)

Where and when would you start to sell everything you have?

Prayer
Lamb of God, you take away the sins of the world, have
mercy on us.

The Ninth Station:
Jesus Falls the Third Time

We adore you O Christ, and we praise you,
because by your Holy Cross, you have redeemed the world.

Meditation: hands of fortitude

The Gospels unfold for us the words and actions of Jesus: He went up the mountain; he called those whom he had chosen; he appointed the twelve to send them to preach, heal and cast out devils; he gave Simon the name 'Peter'; to James the son of Zebedee and John the brother of James he gave the title 'Boanerges', meaning sons of thunder.

In Mark's account of the conversation between Jesus and his disciples at Caesarea Philippi, we read that Jesus came, twice he asked, twice he rebuked, he began to teach, he spoke freely, he turned, he saw the disciples, he spoke to Peter, he called the crowd and he spoke to the crowd. My English teacher in Sligo, Brendan O' Connor, taught me to distinguish between active and passive verbs when reading. It is useful when you read and pray the Gospels.

Here, Jesus is slumped under the Cross. We are not given any indication of Jesus' inward thoughts or outward reactions. Jesus allows himself to be taken and led. Immobile, 'he answered nothing' (Mark 15:5).

Reflection
For by the word of your Son's Gospel
you have brought together one Church
from every people, tongue and nation.
(Eucharistic Prayers For Various Needs – One)

Scripture
Jesus said to him, 'I am the way and the truth and the life. No one comes to the Father except through me'.
(John 14:6)

*When we are lost – Jesus is the Way, before ever
we know his name.
When we search for meaning – Jesus is the Truth that
we can't fully discern.
When death visits us – the Life of Jesus is in our dying breath.*

Prayer
Lamb of God, you take away the sins of the world, have mercy on us.

The Tenth Station:
Jesus Is Stripped of His Garments

We adore you O Christ, and we praise you,
because by your Holy Cross, you have redeemed the world.

Meditation: hands of dependence

Alzheimer's and dementia leaves people waiting patiently upon events around them, as they are the recipients of what happens to them. I met some people in the Nazareth Care Home in Hammersmith who had families, careers and great achievements. Due to severe dementia, disability and bouts of depression, they are confined, restricted and deprived of the power of mobility. These patients embody a contemplative-like silence on beds, their bodies limp and the palms of their hands are opened in wordless prayer. Their posture is one of total dependence. In a way, their beds become altars of offering, where the words 'this is my body' evoke a reality of awe. It leaves an indelible impression that does not diminish human dignity but magnifies it – if we have 'eyes to see'. These people achieved as well as contributed to their families and society. The tenth station helps us to discover how in their passion and patience, no less than in their actions, they bear the likeness of God.

Reflection
Having filled your people with life by the power of your Spirit,
you never cease to gather the whole human race into one.
(Eucharistic Prayers For Various Needs – One)

Scripture
'Ephphatha', that is, 'be opened.'
… he even makes the deaf to hear
and the mute to speak.
(Mark 7:34, 37)

Lord, speak to and rebuke our Church
that locks, closes and excludes.
May rejection never be part of our litany or liturgy.

Prayer
Lamb of God, you take away the sins of the world, have mercy on us.

The Eleventh Station:
Jesus Is Nailed to the Cross

We adore you O Christ, and we praise you,
because by your Holy Cross, you have redeemed the world.

Meditation: hands outstretched

We are created in God's image and likeness. This truth gives us a unique worth. But we can recognise that the image of God is defaced and marred in the lives of those, who by their words and actions do not mirror in their own faces the image of God. We are called to reflect God's image as the core essence of our vocation and the true purpose of our existence. Within the limits of our humanity, we are called to resemble God. This is God's unique gift to us. It is what gives us dignity to the extent that if we fail to resemble God, we blur our human dignity, degrade ourselves and others and lose a precious gift.

In societies where religion is privatised, at times to the level of contempt and resentment, and where attempts are made to sideline and even obliterate God, we lose the innate dignity of every human being as reflections of God's image. The challenge for us today is to rediscover that this dignity belongs to those who are 'nailed' by a system of dependence. It was never more relevant that we recover our shared sense of dignity and worth with all people who feel that they are the last and the least in our society and even in our Church.

Reflection
With mighty hand and outstretched arm
you led you people through the desert.
(Eucharistic Prayer for Various Needs – Two)

Scripture
He told them another parable:
The kingdom of heaven is like yeast that a woman took and mixed
in with three measures of flour until all of it was leavened.
(Matthew 13:33)

A woman knows the hidden secret of God's Word.
It is God who begins in each one of us his own good work.

Prayer
Lamb of God, you take away the sins of the world, have mercy on us.

The Twelfth Station:
Jesus Dies on the Cross

We adore you O Christ, and we praise you,
because by your Holy Cross, you have redeemed the world.

Meditation: hands of sacrifice

When believers and followers of the gospel experience distress,
betrayal, temptation, abandonment or acute physical pain,
it can be a source of comfort and encouragement to them
that, in the words of Cathy, a resident in the Nazareth Care
Home in Hammersmith, 'Jesus knows all about it'. Jesus went
through the same experience of physical and mental suffering.
History tells that Joan of Arc was strengthened in the flames
by the cross of plaited straw held before her eyes. I remember
a young man dying of cancer who, when each injection of

morphine was losing its effect, would slowly move his right hand across his body and cling to the Palm Cross tucked in his pyjama pocket. That Jesus went through pain is a continuing source of both comfort and courage to pain-stricken people. Calvary begins a revolution of the heart in the Centurion who declares, 'In truth this man was the Son of God.' Jesus was not a violent revolutionary or a solitary eccentric. His goal was a change in the hearts and understanding of all people, including the people who exercised political power. All of us are still invited to the way of discipleship.

Reflection
Bring your Church to perfect faith and charity,
and the entire people you have made your own.
(Eucharistic Prayer For Various Needs – Four)

Scripture
Indeed, God did not send the Son into the world to condemn the world
but in order that the world might be saved through him.
(John 3:17)

*The world, the total cosmos is
cherished, beloved, redeemed and saved.*

Prayer
Lamb of God, you take away the sins of the world, have mercy on us.

The Thirteenth Station:
Jesus Is Taken Down from the Cross

We adore you O Christ, and we praise you,
because by your Holy Cross, you have redeemed the world.

Meditation: hands of mercy

Waiting can be the most intense and poignant of all human experiences. Waiting can strip us of affectation, self deception and self-delusion. Jesus prayed that the dreaded cup might pass from him. I remember visiting John, who was severely depressed with a schizophrenic condition. The nurse told me, 'I brought John into the day-room. He is waiting for you there.' John was in the room, but he did not acknowledge me. He looked around with a wandering indifference. Yet, he was not unconscious or unaware of my presence. He called my name once and told me that my coat was wet. John was in a space where nothing mattered. John's condition was pathological, and it led eventually to suicide some months later. The experience of being with John brought home to me that a person can exist with a merely camera-like consciousness, aware of everything but caring about nothing. John perceived the world, but he saw it with a massive indifference, as irrelevant and having no bearing or meaning on himself. John was in a place where waiting was unbearable.

Reflection
He always showed compassion
for children and the poor, for the sick and for sinners
He became a neighbour to the oppressed and the afflicted.
(Eucharistic Prayer For Various Needs – Four)

Scripture
Father, forgive them, for they do not know what they are
doing. (Luke 23:34)

*Forgiveness flows like a healing spring through our
wasted world of excess.
Forgiveness flows seventy-times-seven to saturate
our wounded lives.
Forgiveness heals, cleanses and washes away all our wrongs.*

Prayer
Lamb of God, you take away the sins of the world, have
mercy on us.

The Fourteenth Station:
The Body of Jesus Is Placed in the Tomb

We adore you O Christ, and we praise you,
because by your Holy Cross, you have redeemed the world.

Meditation: anointing hand of tenderness

Jeffrey was homeless for six years. He was a successful lecturer in university. His marriage broke up, and he became addicted to cocaine. He recovered from this addiction only then to find himself thrown out of his family home.

Jeffrey finds dignity not only in his capacity for action as a lecturer but in his capacity to receive and to wait. Others look on him with degradation and derision, but Jeffrey shares with God a secret: the world's power of meaning. The world for him is no mere succession of images recorded and registered in the brain. Jeffrey sees what William Blake saw in his 'Tyger' poem and Immanuel Kant saw in the starry heavens: 'a wonderful terror or a terrifying wonder', to quote him. He has an intense receptivity to the beauty of the ordinary and everyday. He is truly present as he waits, and he waits in a spirit of hope.

Reflection
He is the way that leads to you,
the truth that sets us free,
the life that fills us with gladness.
(Eucharistic Prayer For Various Needs – Three)

Scripture
Was it not necessary that the Messiah should suffer these things
and then enter into his glory?
(Luke 24:26)

Why are we still so slow to believe?
The living God descends among the dead
to bring us new life in broken bread.

Prayer
Lamb of God, you take away the sins of the world, have mercy on us.

Conclusion:
Victorious King, Thy Mercy Show

There is an ancient Latin chant called
the Easter Sequence that dates back to 1048.
It is preserved in the Roman Missal and is known as:
'Victimae paschali laudes immolent Christiani'
Christians, to the Paschal Victim offer praise.

It tells the story of death and life locked in a struggle,
where Christ the Paschal victim is victorious over death.
It tells the story of Mary Magdalene,
who upon finding the empty tomb, proclaims
'Christ my hope has risen'.
It ends with these words:

'That Christ is truly risen from the dead we know;
victorious King, thy mercy show.'

There is richness in this short prayer of praise.
The truth of the Resurrection is stated as a matter of
knowledge and of fact.
It is the great truth that is at the core of our faith,
from which all other truths flow.
It speaks of the victory of Christ the King:
a victory over suffering, a victory over injustice, a victory
over death itself.
It ends with a prayer for mercy.

The prayer is not surprising.
Christ is truly risen.
That is not something that just happened on
one random Sunday morning in a garden and then the world
moved on.
He is risen for you, for me, for all human beings – born and
yet unborn.
This means that we have confidence in approaching him with
all our needs,
knowing that his victory has opened new pathways of life,
pathways that are sure and eternal.

May our prayer for mercy to our risen Lord enfold the people
of Ukraine
and all who have suffered because of the war there.
We conclude with a prayer for the intentions of the Pope.